Armor of God

Written By Angela Gladden

Illustrated By Noelle Frady

WestBow Press books may be ordered through booksellers or by contacting:

WestBow Press
A Division of Thomas Nelson & Zondervan
1663 Liberty Drive
Bloomington, IN 47403
www.westbowpress.com
844-714-3454

Scripture taken from the International Children's Bible®. Copyright © 1986, 1988, 1999 by Thomas Nelson. Used by permission. All rights reserved.

Interior Image Credit: Noelle Frady

ISBN: 978-1-6642-8123-3 (sc)
ISBN: 978-1-6642-8124-0 (e)

Library of Congress Control Number: 2022919856

Print information available on the last page.

WestBow Press rev. date: 10/17/2022

WESTBOW
PRESS®
A DIVISION OF THOMAS NELSON
& ZONDERVAN

This book is dedicated to my nephews and nieces:
Dylan, Avery, Lukas, Jacob, Ainsley, Emily, Samuel,
Alexandria, Margaret, Luna, Ellie, Abigail, & Elias.
They inspired me to write a book for children.

What is armor? Armor is lots of metal pieces that cover the body. Soldiers wear armor when they go into battle.

Why do soldiers need armor? The armor is used to protect their bodies from the enemy during battles.

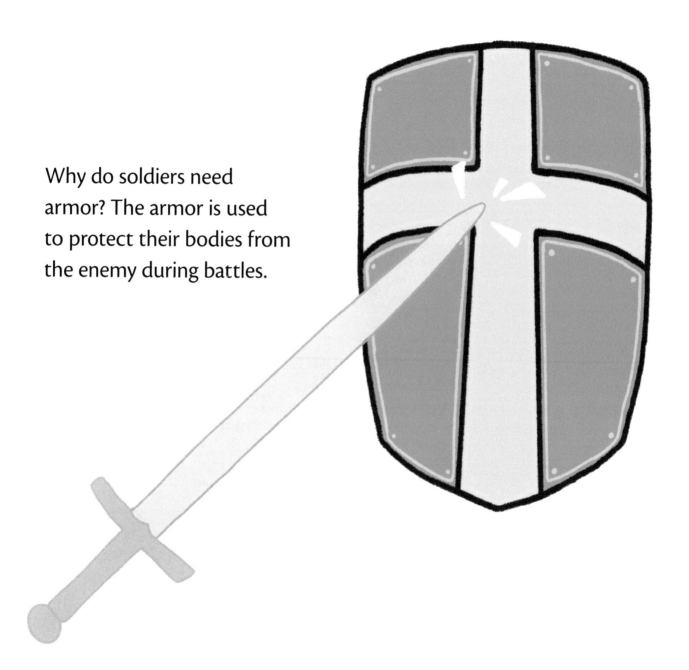

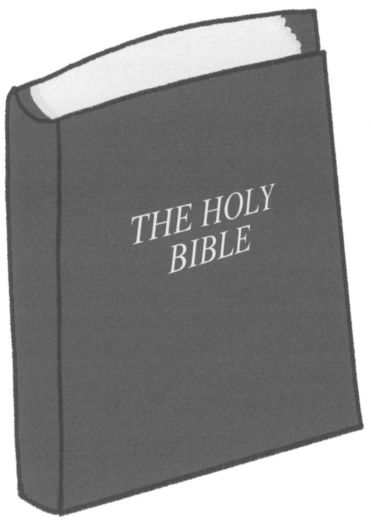

What is the Armor of God? God's armor is made up of spiritual pieces that we can't see. We use the Bible, what we know about God, and our faith to build the armor.

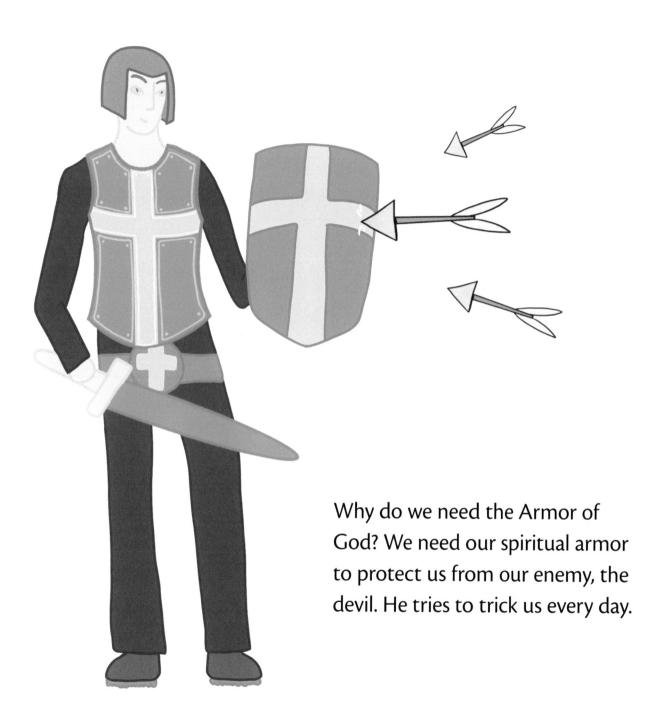

Why do we need the Armor of God? We need our spiritual armor to protect us from our enemy, the devil. He tries to trick us every day.

Wear God's armor so that you can fight against the devil's evil tricks. Ephesians 6:11

The devil is our enemy. He tries to get us to sin like telling lies, cheating and stealing. We wear God's armor to protect us and help us make good choices.

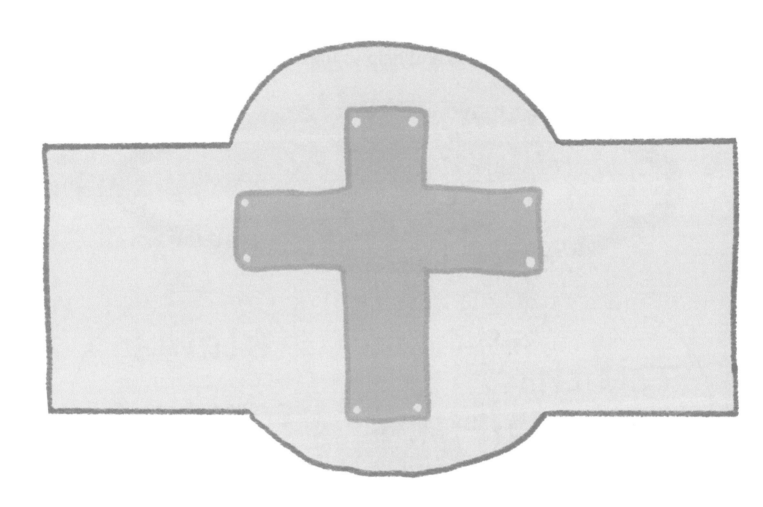

So stand strong, with the belt of truth tied around your waist. Ephesians 6:14a

The belt is used to carry weapons and protect parts of the body from harm. God's belt is the truth of Jesus. We protect ourselves from the devil's evil tricks when we learn about Jesus by reading and remembering Bible verses.

Psalm 119: 11

I have taken your words to heart so I would not sin against you.

And on your chest wear the protection of right living. Ephesians 6:14b

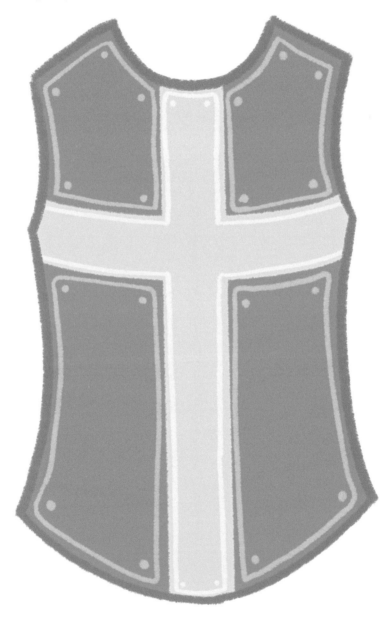

The breastplate is used to protect the heart, lungs
and other organs from harm. God's breastplate is
righteousness through Jesus. We protect our hearts
when we believe Jesus is the son of God, that he
died for our sins and rose from the dead.

And on your feet wear the Good News of peace to help you stand strong. Ephesians 6:15

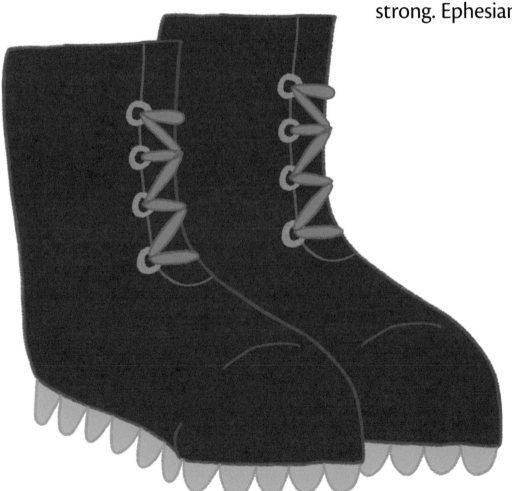

Battle shoes are comfortable and have spikes to help the soldier march long distances and stomp out the enemy. The Good News is that Jesus died on the cross and rose from the dead to pay for our sins. God's shoes help us stand against our enemy, the devil.

And also use the shield of faith. Ephesians 6:16

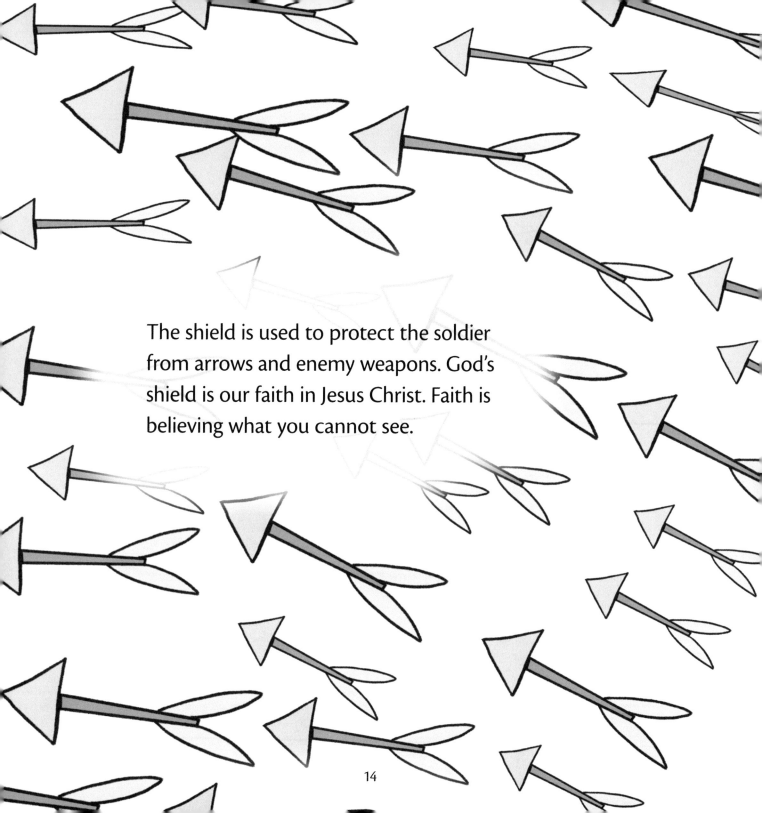

The shield is used to protect the soldier from arrows and enemy weapons. God's shield is our faith in Jesus Christ. Faith is believing what you cannot see.

Accept God's salvation to be your helmet.
Ephesians 6:17a

The helmet protects the soldier's head. We accept
God's salvation when we believe that Jesus is God's son,
who died on the cross for our sins and then God raised
him from the dead. God's helmet protects our minds
and helps us to make good choices.

And take the sword of the Spirit -- that sword is the teaching of God. Ephesians 6:17b

The sword is used for attacking the enemy. God's sword is the Bible. We memorize verses so that we can use His words of truth to attack the devil's lies and tricks.

GOD DID NOT GIVE US A SPIRIT THAT MAKES US AFRAID. HE GAVE US A SPIRIT OF POWER AND LOVE AND SELF-CONTROL. 2 TIMOTHY 1:7

Pray with all kinds of prayers, and ask for everything you need.
Ephesians 6:18

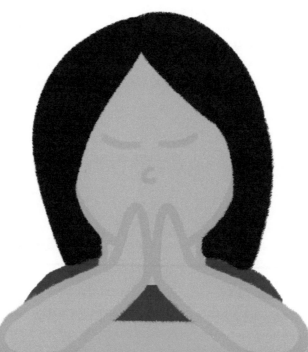

Praying is talking with God. God wants us to thank him, praise him and ask him anything. We can pray out loud or silently at any time. God is always listening.

So don't be afraid. The Lord your God will be with you everywhere you go." Joshua 1:9

We put on the belt, breastplate, shoes, and helmet, carry the shield and sword, and pray always to help us make right choices and to protect us from the devil's evil tricks.

For God so loved the world so much that he gave his only Son. God gave his Son so that whoever believes in him may not be lost, but have eternal life. John 3:16

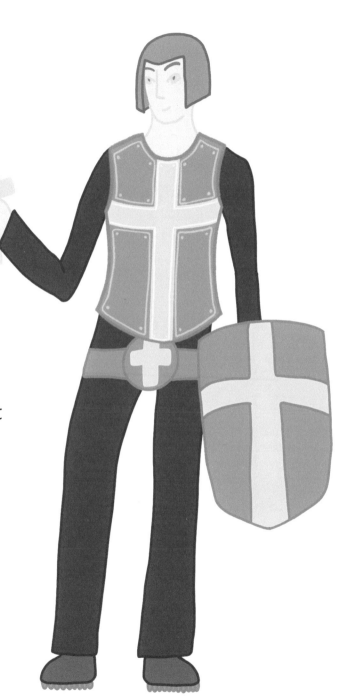

Soldiers use physical armor to protect their bodies during battles. We use God's spiritual armor to protect us from the devil's tricks every day. God loves you and is always with you, so you don't have to be afraid.

Match the name to the armor piece.

Salvation

Faith

God's Word - the Bible

Right Living

Good News Peace

Truth

Prayer

i

Printed in the United States
by Baker & Taylor Publisher Services